GLACIERS
and
ICEBERGS

JENNY MARKERT

THE CHILD'S WORLD

DESIGN
Michael George

PHOTO RESEARCH
Charles Rotter/Archipelago Productions

PHOTO CREDITS
COMSTOCK/Sharon Chester
Ralph Clevenger
E. R. Degginger
Jeff Foott
George Herben
COMSTOCK/Russ Kinne
Lon E. Lauber
Tom & Pat Leeson
Joe McDonald

Library of Congress Cataloging-in-Publication Data
Markert, Jenny.
Glaciers and icebergs / by Jenny Markert.
p.   cm.
Summary: Describes how glaciers and icebergs
form, move, and affect the planet Earth..
ISBN 1-56766-004-5
1. Glaciers--Juvenile literature.
2. Icebergs--Juvenile literature.
[1. Glaciers.   2. Icebergs.]   I. Title.
GB2403.8.M37   1993
551.3'1--dc20   CIP
                                                              AC

Distributed to schools and libraries in the United States by
ENCYCLOPAEDIA BRITANNICA EDUCATIONAL CORP.
310 South Michigan Avenue
Chicago, Illinois 60604

The next time a snowflake lands on your mitten, look at it closely. Notice how easily it's destroyed when you try to pick it up, or how quickly it melts when you breathe on it. Each beautiful snowflake is so fragile! But would you believe that under certain conditions, these gentle, fluffy snowflakes can carve mountains and destroy ocean liners?

Glaciers are enormous rivers of ice—and one of the most powerful forces on our planet. Some glaciers are miles deep and hundreds of miles long! Despite their size and strength, however, glaciers are made up of trillions of tiny, fragile snowflakes, just as trillions of grains of sand make up a beach.

It takes hundreds and sometimes thousands of years for snowflakes to form a glacier. Glaciers are found only where it is extremely cold—atop high mountains and near the North and South Poles. In these places, temperatures are cold all year long. Summers are not warm enough to melt the winter snow, so the snow piles up year after year. As it collects, the snow grows

heavier and thicker. Gradually, the snowflakes are packed tightly together until they form solid, blue ice.

Not just any slab of ice is a glacier, though. To be considered a glacier, the ice must be moving. Glaciers move because they are very heavy, and gravity pulls the ice downhill. The fastest glaciers move about 100 feet each day. How fast a glacier moves is determined by many things. A thick, heavy glacier moves faster because it has its weight pushing it. Steeper slopes and warmer temperatures also cause a glacier to pick up speed. When it is warm, a glacier slides on a slippery layer of water.

Glaciers are so enormous that all the ice cannot move at the same time.

Instead, different parts move at different speeds. The ice in the middle of a glacier usually moves faster than the ice along the sides. Likewise, the ice toward the top often moves faster than the ice along the bottom. The glacier protests loudly, hissing and groaning against all the tugging going on. Some parts snap and buckle from the pressure, leaving ridges and ripples in the ice. Deep, thick cracks called *crevasses* also form. Crevasses sometimes have a thin covering of snow that makes them hard to see. People traveling on glaciers must watch carefully for these crevasses. Falling into one might be like falling into the Grand Canyon—and that's quite a drop!

Glaciers vary greatly in size. *Mountain glaciers* start as snowfields on top of mountains. They creep downward until the ice reaches warmer climates and melts. An *ice cap* is a mountain glacier that has grown big enough to cover the mountain top—like a hat covers your head. A cap of ice wouldn't keep your ears very warm, though, would it?

The largest of all glaciers are called *ice sheets*. They can cover entire mountain ranges, leaving only the tallest peaks showing above the ice. About 15,000 years ago, during the last ice age, ice sheets covered much of North America and Asia. Canada and the northern United States were buried deep under the ice. Gradually, Earth's climate warmed and the ice sheets melted. Today, ice sheets exist only in Antarctica and Greenland—but they hold more ice than all other glaciers combined!

Glaciers, ice caps, and even ice sheets are always changing size. When temperatures are cold and snows are heavy, glaciers grow. The rivers of ice become heavier, thicker, and longer. But when temperatures are above freezing or there is little snowfall, glaciers gradually shrink. The ice melts and the flowing water sculpts a network of tunnels and caves. If temperatures stay warm for many years, a glacier may disappear altogether—just as the ice sheets

that once covered North America and Asia did.

When a glacier melts, it leaves evidence of its former power. In some places, boulders dragged by the flowing ice leave deep scrapes in the ground. In other places, glacial ice and silt polish the underlying rock, producing smooth, rounded rockbeds. The debris carried by a glacier is dropped where the ice melts, leaving piles of rocks, soil, and boulders. Also left is fine glacial silt, which produces rich, fertile soil, such as that covering the farmlands of Iowa and Minnesota.

Glaciers also dig enormous valleys, sometimes leaving lakes of melted ice to fill them in. A valley carved by a glacier is different from one carved by a river. River valleys are shaped like a V, while glacial valleys are shaped like a U. Smaller valleys often hang high above the floors of the largest glacial valleys. Scenic waterfalls, like those in Yosemite National Park, often plummet from these *hanging valleys*.

Some of the evidence glaciers leave behind is much more dramatic than scraped bedrock, glacial silt, or even hanging valleys. When an active glacier lies atop a mountain peak, it slowly rips away pieces of the mountain. Over hundreds of years, it can slowly carve out a bowl-shaped hollow called a *cirque*. If three or four glaciers surround a single peak, they all eat into the mountain

from different sides. The result is a steep, jagged peak called a *horn*. One of the most famous examples is Switzerland's Matterhorn.

Steep-sided coastal inlets called *fjords* are another landmark created by glaciers. Fjords were created ages and ages ago by glaciers that flowed into the sea. When the glaciers eventually retreated, seawater filled the deep valleys left behind. Some of the most beautiful fjords are in Norway and Alaska. The Nordwest Fjord on the east coast of Greenland is 195 miles long!

Even today, there are many places where glaciers meet the sea. In Alaska and Canada hundreds of glaciers flow into the ocean. The ice sheets of Antarctica and Greenland flow out over the water, creating a thick *ice shelf*. Periodically, enormous slabs of ice break off and crash into the sea, producing *icebergs*.

Like glaciers, icebergs exist only where the temperature is extremely cold. They are common only in the Antarctic Ocean and northern regions of the Pacific and Atlantic oceans. Though salty ocean water isn't drinkable, people traveling the oceans can drink the fresh water that melts off icebergs. One day, experts might find a way to use icebergs as water sources for dry lands!

Icebergs come in all different sizes and shapes. Newly formed icebergs can be as tall as skyscrapers and hundreds

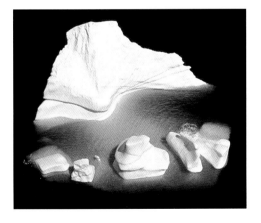

of miles across—more like islands than pieces of ice! Some have flat tops, and others have pointy peaks. Icebergs can be rough and jagged or smooth and polished. Some icebergs have blue streaks running through them, caused by fresh water freezing as it flows through the glacier. No matter what their size, all icebergs eventually disappear as warm seawater laps at their sides and sunshine melts them from above.

Though beautiful, icebergs can be very dangerous to ocean-going ships. A ship can sink very quickly if it bumps into an iceberg! The most famous crash between a ship and an iceberg involved the oceanliner *Titanic*. In 1912, the *Titanic* hit an iceberg and sank to the bottom of the Atlantic Ocean, killing more than 1,500 people.

How can an enormous ocean liner collide with an iceberg? After all, you would think any iceberg big enough to sink a ship must be pretty easy to see! Actually, it is not. The next time you drink a glass of ice water, look at an ice cube. Most of the ice cube lies below the surface of the water. The same is true of an iceberg—only a small part is visible above the surface. For this reason, a good captain knows to steer well clear of icebergs. But sometimes they are impossible to avoid—after all, they can be hundreds of miles across.

As you have learned, icebergs and glaciers have both benefits and hazards. They claim a crucial place in the delicate balance of our planet. The next time it snows, remember that a single snowflake is very fragile—but when combined with trillions of others, it can become a potent force indeed!

INDEX